Muffins & Cupcakes

Everyday recipes to enjoy

blueberry muffins

ingredients

MAKES 12

vegetable oil cooking spray,
  for oiling (if using)
225 g/8 oz plain flour
1 tsp bicarbonate of soda
1/4 tsp salt
1 tsp allspice
115 g/4 oz caster sugar
3 large egg whites
40 g/1 1/2 oz margarine
150 ml/5 fl oz thick low-fat
  natural or blueberry-
  flavoured yogurt
1 tsp vanilla essence
85 g/3 oz fresh blueberries

method

1 Spray a 12-cup muffin pan with vegetable oil cooking spray, or line it with 12 muffin paper cases.

2 Sift the flour, bicarbonate of soda, salt and half of the allspice into a large mixing bowl. Add 6 tablespoons of the caster sugar and mix together.

3 In a separate bowl, whisk the egg whites together. Add the margarine, yogurt and vanilla essence and mix together well, then stir in the fresh blueberries until thoroughly mixed. Add the fruit mixture to the flour mixture, then gently stir until just combined. Do not overstir the mixture – it is fine for it to be a little lumpy.

4 Divide the muffin mixture evenly between the 12 cups in the muffin pan or the paper cases (they should be about two-thirds full). Mix the remaining sugar with the remaining allspice, then sprinkle the mixture over the muffins. Transfer to a preheated oven, 190°C/375°F/Gas Mark 5, and bake for 25 minutes or until risen and golden. Remove the muffins from the oven and serve warm, or place them on a wire rack to cool.

lime & poppy seed muffins

ingredients

MAKES 12

175 ml/6 fl oz sunflower or
groundnut oil, plus extra
for oiling (if using)
225 g/8 oz plain flour
1 tsp baking powder
1/2 tsp salt
225 g/8 oz caster sugar
1 large egg
1 large egg white
150 ml/5 fl oz milk
1 tbsp lime juice
1 tbsp grated lime rind
2 tsp poppy seeds

to decorate

2 tsp grated lime rind
1–2 tsp poppy seeds

method

1 Oil a 12-cup muffin pan with sunflower oil, or line it with 12 muffin paper cases.

2 Sift the flour, baking powder and salt into a mixing bowl. Then add the caster sugar and stir together.

3 In a separate bowl, whisk the egg, egg white, remaining sunflower oil and milk together, then stir in the lime juice and grated lime rind. Add the egg mixture to the flour mixture, then add the poppy seeds and gently stir. Do not overstir the mixture – it is fine for it to be a little lumpy.

4 Divide the muffin mixture evenly between the 12 cups in the muffin pan or the paper cases (they should be about two-thirds full). Sprinkle over grated lime rind and poppy seeds to decorate, then bake in a preheated oven, 190°C/375°F/Gas Mark 5, for 25 minutes or until risen and golden. Serve the muffins warm, or place them on a wire rack to cool.

doughnut muffins

ingredients

MAKES 12

175 g/6 oz butter, softened,
    plus extra for greasing
200 g/7 oz caster sugar
2 large eggs, lightly beaten
375 g/13 oz plain flour
3/4 tbsp baking powder
1/4 tsp bicarbonate of soda
pinch of salt
1/2 tsp freshly grated nutmeg
250 ml/9 fl oz milk

topping

100 g/3 1/2 oz caster sugar
1 tsp ground cinnamon
25 g/1 oz butter, melted

method

1 Grease a deep 12-cup muffin pan. In a large bowl, beat the butter and sugar together until light and creamy. Add the eggs, a little at a time, beating well between additions.

2 Sift the flour, baking powder, bicarbonate of soda, salt and nutmeg together. Add half to the creamed mixture with half of the milk. Gently fold the ingredients together before incorporating the remaining flour and milk.

3 Spoon the mixture into the prepared muffin pan, filling each cup to about two-thirds full. Bake in a preheated oven, 180°C/350°F/Gas Mark 4, for 15–20 minutes or until the muffins are lightly brown and firm to the touch.

4 For the topping, mix the sugar and cinnamon together. While the muffins are still warm from the oven, brush lightly with melted butter, and sprinkle over the cinnamon and sugar mixture. Eat warm or cold.

fruity muffins

ingredients

MAKES 10

275 g/10 oz self-raising
    wholewheat flour

2 tsp baking powder

2 tbsp brown sugar

85 g/3 oz no-soak dried
    apricots, finely chopped

1 banana, mashed with
    1 tbsp orange juice

1 tsp finely grated
    orange rind

300 ml/10 fl oz skimmed milk

1 large egg, beaten

3 tbsp sunflower or
    groundnut oil

2 tbsp rolled oats

fruit spread, honey or maple
    syrup, to serve

method

1 Line 10 cups of a 12-cup muffin pan with muffin paper cases. Sift the flour and baking powder into a mixing bowl, adding any husks that remain in the sieve. Stir in the sugar and chopped apricots.

2 Make a well in the centre and add the mashed banana, orange rind, milk, beaten egg and oil. Mix together well to form a thick mixture and divide the mixture evenly between the muffin cases.

3 Sprinkle with a few rolled oats and bake in a preheated oven, 200°C/400°F/Gas Mark 6, for 25–30 minutes until well risen and firm to the touch or until a toothpick inserted into the centre comes out clean.

4 Remove the muffins from the oven and place them on a wire rack to cool slightly. Serve the muffins while still warm with a little fruit spread, honey or maple syrup.

apple & cinnamon muffins

ingredients

MAKES 6

85 g/3 oz plain wholewheat
    flour

70 g/2 1/2 oz plain white flour

1 1/2 tsp baking powder

pinch of salt

1 tsp ground cinnamon

40 g/1 1/2 oz golden caster
    sugar

2 small eating apples, peeled,
    cored and finely chopped

125 ml/4 fl oz milk

1 egg, beaten

55 g/2 oz butter, melted

topping

12 brown sugar lumps,
    roughly crushed

1/2 tsp ground cinnamon

method

1 Place 6 muffin paper cases in a muffin pan.

2 Sift both flours, baking powder, salt and cinnamon together into a large bowl and stir in the sugar and chopped apples. Place the milk, egg and butter in a separate bowl and mix. Add the wet ingredients to the dry ingredients and gently stir until just combined.

3 Divide the mixture evenly between the paper cases. To make the topping, mix the crushed sugar lumps and cinnamon together and sprinkle over the muffins.

4 Bake in a preheated oven, 200°C/400°F/Gas Mark 6, for 20–25 minutes or until risen and golden. Remove the muffins from the oven and serve warm or place them on a wire rack to cool.

banana pecan muffins

ingredients

MAKES 8

150 g/5½ oz plain flour

1½ tsp baking powder

pinch of salt

70 g/2½ oz golden
caster sugar

115 g/4 oz shelled pecan
nuts, roughly chopped

2 large ripe bananas, mashed

5 tbsp milk

25 g/1 oz butter, melted

1 large egg, beaten

½ tsp vanilla essence

method

1 Place 8 muffin paper cases in a muffin pan. Sift the flour, baking powder and salt into a bowl, add the sugar and pecan nuts and stir to combine.

2 Place the mashed bananas, milk, butter, egg and vanilla essence in a separate bowl and mix together. Add the wet ingredients to the dry ingredients and gently stir until just combined.

3 Divide the mixture evenly between the paper cases and bake in a preheated oven, 190°C/375°F/Gas Mark 5, for 20–25 minutes or until risen and golden. Remove the muffins from the oven and place them on a wire rack to cool.

double chocolate muffins

ingredients

MAKES 12

200 g/7 oz plain flour

25 g/1 oz cocoa powder, plus
    extra for dusting

1 tbsp baking powder

1 tsp ground cinnamon

115 g/4 oz golden caster
    sugar

185 g/6 1/2 oz white chocolate,
    roughly chopped

2 large eggs

100 ml/3 1/2 fl oz sunflower
    or groundnut oil

200 ml/7 fl oz milk

method

1 Line a 12-cup muffin pan with muffin cases.

2 Sift the flour, cocoa, baking powder and cinnamon into a large mixing bowl. Stir in the sugar and 125 g/4 1/2 oz of the white chocolate.

3 Place the eggs and oil in a separate bowl and whisk until frothy, then gradually whisk in the milk. Stir into the dry ingredients until just blended. Divide the mixture evenly between the paper cases, filling each three-quarters full.

4 Bake in a preheated oven, 200°C/400°F/ Gas Mark 6, for 20 minutes or until well risen and springy to the touch. Remove the muffins from the oven, cool in the pan for 2 minutes, then transfer to a wire rack to cool completely.

5 Place the remaining white chocolate in a heatproof bowl, set the bowl over a saucepan of barely simmering water, and heat until melted. Spread over the top of the muffins. Allow to set, then dust the tops with a little cocoa and serve.

chocolate chip muffins

ingredients

MAKES 12

40 g/1¹/₂ oz margarine

200 g/7 oz caster sugar

2 large eggs

150 ml/5 fl oz whole natural
    yogurt

5 tbsp milk

300 g/10¹/₂ oz plain flour

1 tsp bicarbonate of soda

115 g/4 oz plain chocolate
    chips

method

1 Line a 12-cup muffin pan with muffin cases.

2 Place the margarine and sugar in a mixing bowl and beat with a wooden spoon until light and fluffy. Beat in the eggs, yogurt and milk until combined.

3 Sift the flour and bicarbonate of soda into the mixture. Stir until just blended.

4 Stir in the chocolate chips, then divide the mixture evenly between the paper cases and bake in a preheated oven, 200°C/400°F/Gas Mark 6, for 25 minutes or until risen and golden. Remove the muffins from the oven and cool in the pan for 5 minutes, then place them on a wire rack to cool completely.

cranberry cupcakes

ingredients

MAKES 14

75 g/2³/4 oz butter, softened,
   or soft margarine

100 g/3¹/2 oz caster sugar

1 large egg

2 tbsp milk

100 g/3¹/2 oz self-raising flour

1 tsp baking powder

75 g/2³/4 oz cranberries,
   frozen

method

1 Put 14 muffin paper cases in a muffin pan, or place 14 double-layer paper cases on a baking sheet.

2 Put the butter and sugar in a bowl and beat together until light and fluffy. Gradually beat in the egg, then stir in the milk. Sift in the flour and baking powder and, using a large metal spoon, fold them into the mixture. Gently fold in the frozen cranberries. Spoon the mixture into the paper cases.

3 Bake the cupcakes in a preheated oven, 180°C/350°F/Gas Mark 4, for 15–20 minutes or until well risen and golden brown. Transfer to a wire rack to cool.

sticky gingerbread cupcakes

ingredients

MAKES 16

115 g/4 oz plain flour

2 tsp ground ginger

3/4 tsp ground cinnamon

1 piece of preserved
  ginger, finely chopped

3/4 tsp bicarbonate of soda

4 tbsp milk

85 g/3 oz butter, softened,
  or soft margarine

70 g/2 1/2 oz brown sugar

2 tbsp black treacle

2 eggs, lightly beaten

pieces of preserved ginger,
  to decorate

frosting

85 g/3 oz butter, softened

175 g/6 oz icing sugar

2 tbsp ginger syrup from the
  preserved ginger jar

method

1 Put 16 paper baking cases in a muffin pan, or place 16 double-layer paper cases on a baking sheet.

2 Sift the flour, ground ginger and cinnamon together into a bowl. Add the finely chopped ginger and toss in the flour mixture until well coated. In a separate bowl, dissolve the bicarbonate of soda in the milk.

3 Put the butter and sugar in a bowl and beat together until fluffy. Beat in the treacle, then gradually add the eggs, beating well after each addition. Beat in the flour mixture, then gradually beat in the milk. Spoon the mixture into the paper cases.

4 Bake the cupcakes in a preheated oven, 160°C/325°F/Gas Mark 3, for 20 minutes or until well risen and golden brown. Transfer to a wire rack to cool.

5 To make the frosting, put the butter in a bowl and beat until fluffy. Sift in the icing sugar, add the ginger syrup and beat together until smooth and creamy. Slice the preserved ginger into thin slivers or chop finely.

6 When the cupcakes are cold, spread a little frosting on top of each cupcake, then decorate with pieces of ginger.

moist walnut cupcakes

ingredients

MAKES 12

85 g/3 oz walnuts
55 g/2 oz butter, softened
100 g/3$\frac{1}{2}$ oz caster sugar
grated rind of $\frac{1}{2}$ lemon
70 g/2$\frac{1}{2}$ oz self-raising flour
2 eggs
12 walnut halves, to decorate

frosting

55 g/2 oz butter, softened
85 g/3 oz icing sugar
grated rind of $\frac{1}{2}$ lemon
1 tsp lemon juice

method

1 Put 12 paper baking cases in a muffin pan, or place 12 double-layer paper cases on a baking sheet.

2 Put the walnuts in a food processor and, using a pulsating action, blend until finely ground, being careful not to overgrind, which will turn them to oil. Add the butter, cut into small pieces, along with the sugar, lemon rind, flour and eggs, then blend until evenly mixed. Spoon the mixture into the paper cases.

3 Bake the cupcakes in a preheated oven, 190°C/375°F/Gas Mark 5, for 20 minutes or until well risen and golden brown. Transfer to a wire rack to cool.

4 To make the frosting, put the butter in a bowl and beat until fluffy. Sift in the icing sugar, add the lemon rind and juice, and mix well.

5 When the cupcakes are cold, spread a little frosting on top of each cupcake and top with a walnut half to decorate.

frosted peanut butter cupcakes

ingredients

MAKES 16

55 g/2 oz butter, softened,
    or soft margarine
225 g/8 oz brown sugar
115 g/4 oz crunchy
    peanut butter
2 eggs, lightly beaten
1 tsp vanilla essence
225 g/8 oz plain flour
2 tsp baking powder
100 ml/3$\frac{1}{2}$ fl oz milk

frosting

200 g/7 oz full-fat soft
    cream cheese
25 g/1 oz butter, softened
225 g/8 oz icing sugar

method

1 Put 16 muffin paper cases in a muffin pan.

2 Put the butter, sugar and peanut butter in a bowl and beat together for 1–2 minutes, or until well mixed. Gradually add the eggs, beating well after each addition, then add the vanilla essence. Sift in the flour and baking powder and then, using a metal spoon, fold them into the mixture, alternating with the milk. Spoon the mixture into the paper cases.

3 Bake the cupcakes in a preheated oven, 180°C/350°F/Gas Mark 4, for 25 minutes or until well risen and golden brown. Transfer to a wire rack to cool.

4 To make the frosting, put the cream cheese and butter in a large bowl and, using an electric hand whisk, beat together until smooth. Sift the icing sugar into the mixture, then beat together until well mixed.

5 When the cupcakes are cold, spread a little frosting on top of each cupcake, swirling it with a round-bladed knife. Store the cupcakes in the refrigerator until ready to serve.

carrot & orange cupcakes with mascarpone frosting

ingredients

MAKES 12

115 g/4 oz butter, softened,
    or soft margarine

115 g/4 oz brown sugar

juice and finely grated rind of
    1 small orange

2 large eggs, lightly beaten

175 g/6 oz carrots, grated

25 g/1 oz walnut pieces,
    roughly chopped

125 g/4^1/$_2$ oz plain flour

1 tsp ground mixed spice

1^1/$_2$ tsp baking powder

frosting

280 g/10 oz Mascarpone
    cheese

4 tbsp icing sugar

grated rind of 1 large orange

method

1 Put 12 muffin paper cases in a muffin pan.

2 Put the butter, sugar and orange rind in a bowl and beat together until light and fluffy. Gradually add the eggs, beating well after each addition. Squeeze any excess liquid from the carrots and add to the mixture with the walnuts and orange juice. Stir into the mixture until well mixed. Sift in the flour, mixed spice and baking powder and then, using a metal spoon, fold into the mixture. Spoon the mixture into the paper cases.

3 Bake the cupcakes in a preheated oven, 180°C/350°F/Gas Mark 4, for 25 minutes or until well risen, firm to the touch and golden brown. Transfer to a wire rack to cool.

4 To make the frosting, put the Mascarpone cheese, icing sugar and orange rind in a large bowl and beat together until well mixed.

5 When the cupcakes are cold, spread a little frosting on top of each, swirling it with a round-bladed knife. Store the cupcakes in the refrigerator until ready to serve.

lemon butterfly cakes

ingredients

MAKES 12

115 g/4 oz self-raising flour

1/2 tsp baking powder

115 g/4 oz soft margarine

115 g/4 oz caster sugar

2 eggs, lightly beaten

finely grated rind of 1/2 lemon

2 tbsp milk

icing sugar, for dusting

lemon filling

85 g/3 oz butter, softened

175 g/6 oz icing sugar

1 tbsp lemon juice

method

1 Put 12 paper baking cases in a muffin pan, or place 12 double-layer paper cases on a baking sheet.

2 Sift the flour and baking powder into a large bowl. Add the margarine, sugar, eggs, lemon rind and milk and, using an electric hand whisk, beat together until smooth. Spoon the mixture into the paper cases.

3 Bake the cupcakes in a preheated oven, 190°C/375°F/Gas Mark 5, for 15–20 minutes or until well risen and golden brown. Transfer to a wire rack to cool.

4 To make the filling, put the butter in a bowl and beat until fluffy. Sift in the icing sugar, add the lemon juice and beat together until smooth and creamy.

5 When the cupcakes are cold, use a serrated knife to cut a circle from the top of each cupcake and then cut each circle in half. Spread or pipe a little of the buttercream filling into the centre of each cupcake, then press the 2 semicircular halves into it at an angle, to resemble butterfly wings. Dust with a little sifted icing sugar before serving.

feather-iced coffee cupcakes

ingredients

MAKES 16

1 tbsp instant coffee granules

1 tbsp boiling water

115 g/4 oz butter, softened,
    or soft margarine

115 g/4 oz brown sugar

2 eggs

115 g/4 oz self-raising flour

1/2 tsp baking powder

2 tbsp sour cream

icing

225 g/8 oz icing sugar

4 tsp warm water

1 tsp instant coffee granules

2 tsp boiling water

method

1 Put 16 paper baking cases in a muffin pan, or place 16 double-layer paper cases on a baking sheet.

2 Put the coffee granules in a cup or small bowl, add the boiling water and stir until dissolved. Set aside to cool slightly.

3 Put the butter, sugar and eggs in a bowl. Sift in the flour and baking powder, then beat the ingredients together until smooth. Add the dissolved coffee and the sour cream and beat together until well mixed. Spoon the mixture into the paper cases. Bake in a preheated oven, 190°C/375°F/Gas Mark 5, for 20 minutes or until well risen and golden brown. Transfer to a wire rack to cool.

4 To make the icing, sift 140 g/5 oz of the icing sugar into a bowl, then gradually mix in the warm water to make a coating consistency that will cover the back of a wooden spoon. Dissolve the coffee granules in the boiling water. Sift the remaining icing sugar into a bowl, then stir in the dissolved coffee granules. Spoon the icing into a piping bag fitted with a fine nozzle. When the cupcakes are cold, coat the tops with the white icing, then quickly pipe the coffee icing in parallel lines on top. Using a skewer, draw it across the piped lines in both directions. Allow to set before serving.

This edition published in 2013
LOVE FOOD is an imprint of Parragon Books Ltd

Parragon
Chartist House
15–17 Trim Street
Bath, BA1 1HA, UK

Copyright © Parragon Books Ltd 2008

LOVE FOOD and the accompanying heart device is a registered trade mark of Parragon Books Ltd in Australia, the UK, USA, India and the EU.

www.parragon.com/lovefood

ISBN: 978-1-4723-0574-9

Printed in China

Notes for the Reader

This book uses both metric and imperial measurements. Follow the same units of measurement throughout; do not mix metric and imperial. All spoon measurements are level: teaspoons are assumed to be 5 ml, and tablespoons are assumed to be 15 ml. Unless otherwise stated, milk is assumed to be full fat, eggs and individual vegetables are medium, and pepper is freshly ground black pepper. Unless otherwise stated, all root vegetables should be washed in plain water and peeled prior to using.

Garnishes, decorations and serving suggestions are all optional and not necessarily included in the recipe ingredients or method.

The times given are an approximate guide only. Preparation times differ according to the techniques used by different people and the cooking times may also vary from those given. Optional ingredients, variations or serving suggestions have not been included in the time calculations.

Recipes using raw or very lightly cooked eggs should be avoided by infants, the elderly, pregnant women, convalescents and anyone suffering from an illness. Pregnant and breastfeeding women are advised to avoid eating peanuts and peanut products. Sufferers from nut allergies should be aware that some of the ready-made ingredients used in the recipes in this book may contain nuts. Always check the packaging before use.